A Report on the College Board Colloquium

Is This What It's Come To —
Winner Take All?

Joseph Allen, *vice provost for Enrollment, University of Southern California*

Sharon Alston, *director of College Counseling, The Bullis School*

Edwin Below, *project manager, Student and Faculty Information System, Wesleyan University*

Steven Brooks, *executive director, North Carolina State Education Assistance Authority*

Linda Clement, *assistant vice president and director of Undergraduate Admissions, University of Maryland*

Youlonda Copeland-Morgan, *associate vice president of Admission and Financial Aid, Harvey Mudd College*

Georgette DeVeres, *director of Financial Aid, Claremont McKenna College*

Carolyn Lindley, *director of Financial Aid, Northwestern University*

Jerry Lucido, *director of Admission, University of North Carolina, Chapel Hill*

Robert J. Massa, *dean of Enrollment, Johns Hopkins University*

Barry McCarty, *dean of Enrollment Services, Lafayette College*

James Miller, *director of Financial Aid, Harvard and Radcliffe Colleges*

Michael Nettles, *professor of Education, University of Michigan*

Paul Orehovec, *vice provost and dean of Enrollment, University of Miami*

Bernard Pekala, *director of Financial Strategies, Boston College*

Bruce Poch, *dean of Admissions, Pomona College*

Janet Lavin Rapelye, *dean of admission, Wellesley College*

Donald A. Saleh, *dean of Admission and Financial Aid, Cornell University*

Joellen Silberman, *dean of Enrollment, Kalamazoo College*

Rod Skinner, *director of College Counseling, Shorecrest Preparatory School*

Catherine Thomas, *associate dean of Enrollment Services and director of Financial Aid, University of Southern California*

Barbara E. Tornow, *executive director of Financial Assistance, Boston University*

Last but not least, thanks are due to College Board staff members Kathleen Little, executive director of Financial Aid Services, and Clavel Camomot and Tara Brown, staff assistants, for their roles in the planning and implementation of the colloquium, and to Deb Thyng Schmidt, consultant to the College Scholarship Service®, for her assistance in the preparation of this report.

Hal Higginbotham
Vice President
Student Assistance Services

Welcoming Comments

Donald A. Saleh, dean of admissions and financial aid at Cornell University and chair of the College Scholarship Service Council, opened the 1999 colloquium by welcoming all the attendees and presenters and by thanking especially Ed Below (project manager, student/faculty information system, Wesleyan University), who chairs the Financial Aid Standards and Services Committee, and Georgette DeVeres (associate dean and director of financial aid, Claremont McKenna College), who serves as chair-elect of the College Scholarship Service Council, for their "wonderful efforts to put together what I am sure will be a valuable colloquium."

Saleh said, "I am delighted to see so many of you here, and I thank you for taking the time to share with each other your ideas and concerns as we try to work in a winner-take-all environment. We are under constant pressure to do better: to handle the competition better, to have better aid strategies, to bring in more applications. At the same time, families, students, and counselors are under increasing pressure to be 'winners' in the process." Saleh expressed hope that the discussions over the following two days would provide a background for consensus in dealing with the pressures of the enrollment and financial aid arenas. Saleh then introduced Donald M. Stewart, president of the College Board, thanking him and all those at the College Board and the College Scholarship Service—especially Kathleen Little, executive director, Financial Aid Services—who helped to make the colloquium a reality.

Donald Stewart welcomed the participants on behalf of the College Board and expressed delight with the "cross-section of the professions represented among the attendees." Stewart indicated that dialogue between public and private institutions is very important, and that apparently these two sectors in higher education are increasingly recognizing their common concerns. He stated that the College Board is happy "to provide a vehicle for discussion of important issues."

In reading materials in preparation for this colloquium, Stewart found himself "overwhelmed by the amount of detail that is part of your professional lives. The government is dictating a lot of what you do, and

this is enormously intrusive, or at the very least, very influential."
He went on to say that, "in the compliance-driven, detail-oriented
environment in which financial aid professionals work, it is important
to have the opportunity for intellectual exchange on moral and ethical
issues." Such exchanges help to put back some of the "romance" that
has been missing from the work.

Stewart ended his remarks by reiterating his welcome to all attendees,
and assuring them that he was confident that "we will all learn a lot from
this important gathering." ■

Can Need-Based Financial Aid Survive in a Winner-Take-All Environment?

T he keynote address for the colloquium was given by Robert H.
Frank, Goldwin Smith Professor of Economics, Ethics, and Public
Policy at Cornell University. His remarks were based on two of
his books: *The Winner Take All Society* (cowritten with Philip Cook) and
Luxury Fever: Money and Happiness in an Era of Excess.

Professor Frank set the stage by pointing out that the market for
education services is not a standard market, in that, in a textbook-case
market, a price is set where supply and demand meet. In education,
especially at the high-quality liberal arts colleges, "demand far exceeds
supply." Frank referred to a "representative college" in the East, where
4,500 students typically apply for 500 available places in a freshman
class; the price that is charged for the education at that institution is
only about one-third of the total cost to produce it, so a $20,000 annual
price tag comes with an education that actually takes $65,000 to produce
each year. "This isn't the way it is for private sector firms that produce
goods for sale in the marketplace."

Another difference in the education market, Frank pointed out, is that
hierarchy matters more in the education market than in textbook-case
markets, and this hierarchy is becoming ever more important. There
has been a fundamental change in the past 25 years in the payoff to
getting an elite education. Education at the top schools has steadily
transformed into a "winner-take-all" market. In such markets, there is
not always just one winner, but several—but there are very few winners
in such markets in relation to the total number of contestants. Frank
shared that, "These types of markets, while they have existed in narrow
arenas in the past, are spreading more widely across the economy."

Frank indicated that entertainment and sports have historically been
markets that operated in this way. In these markets, in recent history,
there has been a major difference in economic reward to participants,
and technology has a lot to do with it. He used as an example the fact
that a hundred years ago, almost every town had some sort of opera or

live music concert hall, and people would come to hear any one of hundreds of traveling sopranos. The "best" soprano could not supply all the demand, so there was great demand for many good sopranos, not necessarily just the best. "Now, most music we listen to is recorded.... It is Kathleen Battle vs. all other sopranos, and since her performances are available to anyone on CD, why would people pay to hear the second-best soprano?" So there is a very big difference in financial reward between the winner (Miss Battle) and the losers (all other sopranos), even though there might not be much difference between them in terms of talent.

Frank went on to explain that this "winner-take-all" phenomenon is occurring in several other markets now as well. He presented the example of income tax preparation. It used to be that taxes were done by local experts. Then came H&R Block® franchises, "which grabbed an enormous share of the tax-preparation market." Next came tax software, which originally offered hundreds of options. Now Turbotax® has virtually captured this market; it is seen as the "best" and "makes the major share of money in this market, having been anointed the 'best' by the critics." Technology allows us to clone the best and distribute it widely. Frank referred to "plowback," the fact that once a product is perceived as the "best," many more people will buy it.

The income tax preparation evolution process has been paralleled by the competition between the Mac® and Windows® platforms. Now that Windows is considered the operating system of choice, buyers are putting their money there, even in instances where by most accounts the Mac operating system had been considered the superior option. In some places where Macs have been preferred—like Frank's campus— support is being withdrawn because it is too expensive to provide support for two systems. "Once Windows achieved numerical superiority, that in and of itself made it the platform of choice."

Another aspect of the winner-take-all payoff structure is that "in many markets, what we care about is not the product itself but how it compares with other products like it." As an example, Frank pointed out

that in buying an automobile, consumers take basic characteristics for granted; buyers are looking for something more and compare vehicles on characteristics that are "positional" in nature: speed, looks, prestige, rarity. He asked participants to suppose a consumer was deciding between a Porsche® 911 Turbo at $105,000 and a Ferrari® 456 GT at $207,000. "How would you choose? In terms of functional characteristics, there is not a compelling case to be made, even independent of price.... Why would anyone buy the Ferrari? It is not as fast, doesn't have as much grip, breaks down more often, and costs more to repair. Why? Because it's more *rare*.

"So positioning has become extremely important to firms, and that's a setup for winner-take-all: only 10 percent of products can be in the top 10 percent." Because the market rewards have become greater in a winner-take-all scenario, businesses want to be known as the best—the *best* consulting firm, for example—or known to hire only the best (movie producers). Wanting to be the best provides a powerful incentive for these firms to hire the best, and if they are positioned as the best, they can attract and hire the best people. This is "fundamentally different from ordinary markets: McKinsey® needs the elite management consulting recruits as much as the elite management consulting recruit needs McKinsey."

Frank then shared with the group how the winner-take-all market forces are affecting education. There is increasing pressure on students to matriculate at the top colleges and universities, in order to get into the top grad and professional schools, in order ultimately to get into the best firms.

"We see a variety of practices that I describe under the general rubric of the 'positional arms race' occurring earlier and earlier." Frank described the increased "kindergarten redshirting" of boys, keeping them back a year before entering kindergarten so that they will be better able to face competition, be more confident, more successful athletically, and eventually more likely to gain admission to an elite college. "If everybody holds kindergartners out an extra year, none of these goals are served; if we have seven- and eight- and nine-year-old kindergartners, it becomes foolish." State school systems try to solve the problem by taking collective action to limit kindergarten redshirting; almost every state has what Frank terms "a positional arms control agreement" to outlaw redshirting by having a set birthdate deadline. There is much more efficiency with that regulation than without it. "This metaphor of kindergarten redshirting describes to some degree what we are confronting in the admissions and aid sectors now."

In terms of college, there has been a "vastly greater funneling of the 'best' students into the elite schools." Frank related that those students who score over 700 on the verbal portion of the SAT® have been much more concentrated each decade into the "top" schools (those rated most or highly selective by Barron's®). And this generates a feedback loop: As more of the top students go to these schools, the payoffs get ever higher.

Frank explained that, in a major difference from other markets, in education, "your customers are also your input: They help produce your service." Frank referred to a study showing that students deciding where to go to college indicated that, all things being equal, they would want to be where the average student's SAT scores were 100 points higher than their own; "a reverse Lake Woebegon effect."

In addition to this feedback loop, there are payoffs in terms of opportunities for graduates. Frank indicated that more and more elite firms are looking only at graduates of the top-ranked institutions. One way firms can shore up their position is to be able to say that they hire only graduates from top-ranked institutions. This philosophy is now also pervading the faculty ranks, as the top new doctorates know the rankings and want to congregate at the top schools, where they perceive the best students to be.

"All of this sets up *enormous* pressure to bid for all the resources that help you command a top spot in the institutional pecking order." Top schools can get the best students, the best faculty, the most NSF funding, and thus certify their position as an elite school, insuring

"In principle, there's a remedy; whether in practice it's very promising is another question," Frank concluded. "There is a *vast* amount of waste out there; we are satisfying individual interests, but it makes no sense from a social perspective." ■

Do Traditional Institutional Quality Measures (Acceptance Rates, Yield Rates, Win Rates) Really Measure Quality?

D on Saleh introduced this panel discussion by asking the group, "How much of the pressure we feel comes from ourselves? When we engage in a constant comparison of our efforts with those at other institutions on the basis of traditional measures, such as test scores, rank in class, yield and win rates, we accede to the pressurized environment. Are these measures the ones we should constantly be talking about? Do they truly serve the best interests of our students and our institutions?"

Janet Lavin Rappelye, dean of admissions at Wellesley College and College Board trustee, began by asking, "Do our institutional quality measures really measure quality? How well do these measures work?" When she goes before her trustee board, she characterizes a class by such measures as the accept rate, yield, SAT scores, rank in class, and some hints at diversity and special talents. "All of these attributes form an image of a class for the outside world," but the intangibles, "such as creativity and motivation," cannot truly be measured. Rappelye admitted, "I would like to put a disclaimer on the profile like that on mutual fund materials: 'Please remember, past performance does not always predict future success.'" Students come in with "star qualities" and we try to nurture them; how can we get a message to the public that they are more than just the statistics?

Rappelye first addressed the standard diversity measures. She indicated that affirmative action allows for planning and learning from the past—"but the downside is that it allows opponents of affirmative action to look at the statistics and make their own assumptions." She also asserted that "we need to work on the categories so that students can say who they are" as opposed to imposing on them narrow definitions of racial or ethnic heritage. "Multiracial students don't fit into the old categories," and the statistics we capture by using the timeworn categories are "woefully inadequate" as true measures of a class.

He went on to describe a widening gap between those on the college side and those on the secondary school side: early programs contribute to conflicts between secondary school and college admission counselors. Allen indicated that access to the best schools is accelerated for those who are not disadvantaged, and early decision requires counselors to do their work earlier and interferes with their ability to help students who truly need longer to prepare. In addition, students are not encouraged to explore their options and get to know themselves better, because early decision programs compress the whole process. He is concerned that the whole philosophy behind National Association for College Admission Counseling (NACAC) efforts to give students the whole senior year to explore and decide is set aside by early decision programs. "This is not a process set up to help students, but to help institutions. I can't think of a better example of a winner-take-all strategy."

Next, Allen proposed a possible solution. He suggested the participants "step back and take a good look at the process, perhaps declaring a three-year moratorium on the use of early models." He suggested participants look at the data and determine what the effect of proliferating early decision programs has been (early indications would be that the winners are primarily white, upper–middle-class males). He urged that participants work "to discover in a real way, with a research agenda, what early decision really brings us. We may decide it is a necessary or at least OK facet of what we do. But at the very least, we should consider reducing the number of models that exist from nine or so to one or two."

He suggested this could also help answer the question that many secondary school counselors have: "Is our profession capable of regulating itself? If we undertake a review of early decision programs, we can help address the power imbalance between high school and college counselors, and will show our wider audiences that we are capable taking a hard look at our own practices and the effects of what we do collectively." Allen concluded that if the moratorium proposal seems impossible, at least a joint commission put together by NACAC and the College Board should be established to study the issue.

Sharon Alston, director of college counseling at the Bullis School, then provided a secondary school counselor's perspective. She shared with the group that, despite years of experience as an admissions officer, she was "completely unprepared for the lengths to which families would go to try to alleviate stress in the college admission process. Parents are not evil, but they will use every strategy available to help their kids 'win'."

Although Alston said that "on the surface" early decision programs seem like a win-win strategy, she is convinced that these programs work to impact negatively students, parents, counselors, and even the climate of a school. There is a "panic that if you don't apply early, you won't get in. Teenagers are not known for their foresight or decisiveness, but early decision forces this." With time and guidance, Alston stated, students can ultimately make good decisions and learn about themselves, prioritize their goals and values, and decide which institutions will best meet their needs—but early decision "undermines the self-discovery process." Early decision is no longer viewed as an option for the rare student but as another strategy to "get the process over with."

As for counselors, early decision programs add to the level of stress, according to Alston. She indicated that at some schools, more than 50 percent of the seniors are applying early; indeed, at Bullis, the percentage has grown from 10 to 50 percent in the past six years (and at a nearby school, 90 percent of the seniors applied early). "I worry about the quality of service we can give students when they need to get their applications to the counseling office by October." She expressed concern that, with so much attention going to the early decision students, "what attention is going to the students who need more time?" She also reminded the group that seniors can grow, change, and mature a great deal from the end of the junior year and throughout the senior year, and that in many ways they are different people with different goals even a few months further into the process.

Alston also indicated that early decision affects the whole school climate in a way in which many admissions officers are unaware. When so many

students are admitted to college early, the importance of the senior year is lessened. She shared a quotation from a recent article in *The Journal of College Admissions*, likening the senior year these days to Newark Airport: "No one wants to be there, but they have to go through it to get where they're going." Faculty are trying to get students to wrestle with ideas when the students have already "checked out." This severe senior slump "poisons the atmosphere for everyone still invested in the educational process." And the students who were not admitted early add to the stress the regular decision applicants feel: "If they didn't get in, what are my chances?" It also shakes students' and families' faith in the counselor.

Alston went on to express concern that early decision programs work to the advantage of students who are not concerned about financial aid. For those students who are admitted for whom aid *is* a concern, aid packages are often less generous than they might be, because the students are seen by the colleges as already "in the pocket." Another concern is that early decision has become confusing: "There are now at least ten models, each with its own deadlines, options, and terminology." Families and counselors are legitimately upset by the lack of congruity.

In conclusion, Alston stated that "equity is the issue at the center of the early decision debate." She expressed disappointment that "All of this applies to a relatively small number of colleges and students from the perspective of higher education as a whole; it is a major issue for this audience, but what about others?" She shared with the group that in Washington, D.C., there are some public schools where two-thirds of the students take no college admission standardized tests. In Baltimore, some schools don't have enough desks—but it "works out" eventually because some 50 percent of students are likely to drop out before graduation. "The have-nots keep *not* getting." She would like to see the participants "broaden our definition of education, wherein everyone will have the opportunity to contribute to society."

Bruce Poch, dean of admissions at Pomona College, opened his remarks by asking where all this confusion and controversy came from; "Early decision used to be a win-win proposition, but now that has changed and everyone is feeling a loss of control." Poch indicated that part of the change has come about because of the proliferation of information and misinformation in the past 15 to 20 years. "We are all held accountable for what is in *USA Today, U.S. News and World Report,* on the Web, and the rest."

Poch feels that early decision began to mutate because, in the face of this pressure and scrutiny, "admissions officers wanted more control over yield, and treasurers wanted more control over finances." And while high percentages of early decision admits in a freshman class are not new, they are definitely on the rise in general, and this makes students and families nervous. Poch admitted that "collegiality is breaking down; early decision is a way to go to war with your institution's competitors in the rankings."

But he also cautioned that "there is very powerful consumer demand" for early decision, so he would not recommend doing away with it. "There should be a rational way to limit some of the problems" such as early decision admit percentages above 45 or 50 percent and unfair treatment in financial aid packaging. Poch believes, "We should be able to come up with a common glossary and be more aware of the have-nots. There is a way to do early decision 'right' and create a winners' environment rather than a win/lose environment. We need to work responsibly so that we don't trap kids in the middle and we don't leave secondary school counselors on the outside."

Jim Miller then asked the panelists if there is a logical point that is definitely too early to apply to college. He had heard of a college that encouraged students to apply at the end of their junior year (not just programs for early admission of students who have exhausted the offerings of their high school). Bruce Poch said he is concerned about tuition prepayment plans that create investment in a particular college while the students are still in grade school; he also feels there would be no way for counselors to handle the process any earlier than it already takes place. Sharon Alston agreed that logistically it would not be manageable. Joe Allen said that there are so many other aspects of

and consulting economist to Financial Aid Standards and Services Advisory Committee) in the latest issue of the *College Board Review* that "efficiency and equity can be not only compatible, but that they represent complementary principles in the allocation of financial aid."

Stewart admitted, "I don't have a comprehensive cure for what ails us in higher education, but let me suggest at least three elements of a prescription:

- "First, we should *choose to engage in the struggle* to make education better—for all students. This is...a matter of believing in our young people.... It is impressing accountability outcomes on K-12, not for political reasons or to satisfy some invidious investment calculus, but for the sake of the children who will benefit from those high standards. It also means adopting accountability outcomes for our own institutions of higher education as a reciprocal measure, in part as recognition of society's trust in us, but more to insure that we serve these students well....

- "Second, we should *choose to be fair....* The fact is that we work for protected institutions, and fairness—i.e., concern for the larger world—is an essential part of the social compact on which we rely and to which we must contribute.... Society exempts us from [some pressures] precisely because we do something special for society and its young people...we *owe* something to society in return for these privileges.

- "Finally, we have every reason to *refuse to choose* between those values that ought not to be separated. Just as Sandy Baum tells us we don't have to choose between equity and interdependent efficiency, we don't have to choose between equity and educational excellence.... Moral imperative and enlightened self-interest make it possible and necessary for us to hold both values dear and to drive toward them both, not toward one at the exclusion of the other."

In conclusion, Stewart stated that we are "educators...the people who see the power of learning to change the lives of our children. In a democratic society so in need of intellectual sustenance, we work to liberate lives by the freeing of minds.... That is one very right thing we can now do, for whatever the economic world, in the end, we want to build a system in which all participants can win." ∎

may be true, it doesn't relieve us from responsibility to find new ways to provide and protect need-based aid in the current environment. We can't just passively accept these tendencies of society." She mentioned the new proposed Institutional Methodology as a way to focus on a family's ability to pay rather than their willingness to pay.

Copeland-Morgan also expressed her concern that "So much of our energy is focused on the top 20 percent of our society. We need to widen our discussions to see who the losers are."

In closing, Copeland-Morgan shared the following quotation from Sandy Baum's article: "Our role has to be to contribute to the forces of equity in society, to strengthen the role of higher education, its character both as a social institution and as a shaper of individual members of society. We cannot afford not to maintain and work for increased equity and access, just as we can't afford to cut costs by decimating the curriculum, ignoring faculty-student interaction, or failing to offer high-quality education. The objective of enrollment management has to be to strengthen the institutional financial position in order to allow us to achieve our educational goals. We cannot allow the process to cause us to abandon these goals."

Paul Orehovec, vice provost at the University of Miami, spoke next. He expressed his confidence that Sandy Baum's theory will work, and will work primarily "because of you, the participants.... The traditional financial aid professional is the greatest advocate for equity and need-based aid that we have ever seen—and you won't let it go away." But he went on to say that the "greatest weakness in how we get from where we are to where we have to go is you," in that financial aid professionals "see things in a different way than others in the process do."

For example, he said that "financial aid leveraging is a misnomer; it is simply optimizing net revenue. It's simply a pricing issue and it has always been there" in the aid process. He then asked, "Did every government program have the interests of students in mind?" He would argue that the G.I. Bill and the plethora of financial aid programs were

developed primarily to serve political ends. It "is in politicians' interest
to get money into the hands of middle-income kids; we are the ones
who worked to help the truly needy kids, and we will continue to work to
do so."

Orehovec went on to list the six factors economists would say influence
education purchasing decisions:

· price of education

· family's available income

· family's accumulated wealth

· price of other family products and services

· tastes and preferences of the family

· family's expectation of future income, wealth, and prices

"The first four of these factors are the basis of need analysis, the
family's ability to pay; the final two deal with willingness to pay. These
are no different than they were in the 1950s. The *students* who are going
to college are different, because we've put so much focus on ability to
pay—and we will not stop that. It's critical for us. "

Orehovec went on to say that "every institution has its own demand
curve; the idea of doing a pricing model is not 'bad.'" He believes the
only reason such models are more common these days is that the
technology exists to do such projections easily and quickly. "Enrollment
management is a synergistic process, not an evil force.... It is the
involvement of a variety of administrators together to do research, make
a plan, implement, and assess it; it is not primarily about getting
students to come to your school instead of another. If we could do this
not just within our campuses but as a group of higher education
administrators together, it would be better for students."

He then questioned, "Is financial aid owned by the financial aid

profession itself? The profession has a long history of seeing itself as helping students come to college based on family ability to pay." But everyone has a different perspective on financial aid: Admissions sees it as a way to get students to enroll; faculty see it as a reward to good students; budget officers see it as a means to get revenue. "How do presidents, provosts, trustees, and coaches see it? How do the federal and state governments see aid?" Orehovec would argue that *only* financial aid people see aid as primarily helping needy students.

Orehovec then raised a number of other questions: What is the difference between a decrease in tuition and a discount rate? What if we were to reduce the tuition by 10 to 15 percent for everyone? Is the demand curve the same for all departments within a college or university? "We talk about *process* at conferences, but not what works, what the *outcomes* are. We can use market research and other elements of enrollment management to the advantage of the neediest students."

He concluded, "We have to ask ourselves the question, 'What have I done lately?'" Participants need to recognize the importance of enrollment management tools and use them to assist the neediest students. "Your advocacy, not the technology, will make the difference in keeping your institution focused on equity."

The audience then had a chance for comments and questions. Kathy Osmond commented that she was grappling with the issues of equity, leveraging, and the like. "One of my conclusions is that whatever policies we have, they must be fully disclosed...and their disclosure can drive the creation of ethical policies. Secondly, our faculty...do promote equity and justice, and we need to find ways to network with them and use them as allies."

Phil Wick said that "The reality of need-based versus merit aid is that, in the past ten years in particular, we have seen the growth of merit or discount aid at the *expense* of need-based aid. We need to move beyond institutional definitions of equity and toward a wider community definition." Copeland-Morgan agreed that this is a big concern. She suggested, "The definition should initiate from the institution, but the test comes from reaction to disclosure of the policy by the wider community."

Jim Belvin expressed his concern about "a subtle but increasingly important shift in families' willingness to pay. Merit scholarships, like guns, aren't inherently bad. But merit scholarships *invariably* come at the expense of need-based aid. So if enrollment management's goal is *not* to bring a student in as opposed to his or her going to another school, why keep upping the ante?" Orehovec responded, "Competition is not bad, and pricing is part of it. Enrollment management should be primarily research and used to develop models that put institutions in a position to help needy students.... Merit aid, if it takes away from needy kids, is bad—but done right, it might bring in more money that could be used to help needy students." ■

What Are the
Unintended Consequences of a
Winner-Take-All Society?
What Can We Do About Them?

Georgette DeVeres, director of financial aid at Claremont McKenna College and vice-chair of the CSS® Council, moderated this panel. She said that the panelists would help to provide some focus and perspective for the future, based on all that the participants had heard over the past two days. She stated her belief that "We have truly come full circle from when financial aid professionals and CSS first came together to create a formula for need-based aid distribution. We have moved from the policies of choice and access to the policy of rewarding the 'haves'; from need-based aid to, as Steve Brooks calls it, 'greed-based' aid. We need to take back ownership of the definitions of quality measures, both as institutions and collectively." She indicated that it is time to focus again on the greater good of society, to keep the gap from widening, and to once more "build a system wherein all participants can win."

Linda Clement, assistant vice president and director of undergraduate admissions at the University of Maryland and a College Board trustee, followed up DeVeres's comments by agreeing that "our roles have changed. What was right for my institution used to be what was right for prospective students; it was a 'win-win' situation. College colleagues were colleagues, not competitors; college counselors were also colleagues, not clients; prospective students were students, not customers; and financial aid officers and policies were not a focus of controversy. This changing of roles is, as I see it, the great unintended consequence of the winner-take-all society."

Clement offered some suggestions as to where participants might "go from here" in terms of admission practices:

- We should collectively take control of the measures we use to define success.

- We need to give greater focus to the "best fit" in college transition, and by "best fit" we mean both academic and financial fit.

- We need to find better ways to define quality, using measures that aren't necessarily quantitative.

- We need to commit to diversity. We need to find new ways to do research to help us defend what we do, celebrate our success in increasing diversity, and commit to further increasing diversity.

- We should use the College Board associational structure (assemblies) to self-regulate (admissions conventions, etc.).

- We should join forces to exert our leadership in affecting the federal and state agenda.

Barbara Tornow, executive director of financial assistance at Boston University, spoke next about what she sees as the major unintended consequence of the winner-take-all society as it relates to financial aid: "There has been a loss of equity—and there has been a loss of *concern* about the loss of equity." She indicated that there are "real threats" to the viability of need-based aid: For example, more money is going to elite students, merit scholarships are taking away award money from the neediest students, and the government is "bailing out" of financial aid programs for the neediest students. In the face of all this, participants should consider that:

- We need to do a better job providing early information and encouragement to low-income students and their families; we need to inspire students to consider higher education as a real possibility.

- We should provide better information to families and counselors about how to compare and evaluate financial aid awarding policies, and should inform students clearly about how Early Decision (ED) admission may limit their ability to get the fullest financial aid consideration.

- We need to educate others at our institutions about the efficiency of our need-based aid approach.

- We need to support the new Institutional Methodology proposal from FASSAC to move toward greater consensus.

- We need to develop media campaigns to reemphasize the principle that paying for college is the responsibility first of the parents and student, but that financial aid is there for those who are unable to pay. ■

Winner-Take-All Markets and Need-Based Financial Aid

Keynote Address by Robert H. Frank

The Keynote Address was edited by the speaker in preparation for publication, and does not match exactly the remarks as quoted and summarized on pages 5-13.

In preparing for this talk I came across a passage in which economist Gordon Winston said that buyers in the market for higher education confront a decision more like a one-shot investment in a cancer cure than shopping for groceries. I believe Winston's remark actually understates the difference between the typical market described in textbooks and the market for higher education. Shopping for groceries and shopping for a cancer cure in fact have far more in common with each other than with shopping for a spot in an American university.

If grocers or oncologists charge inflated fees, their high earnings will attract competitors who will drive prices back down. But that's not the way things work at all in the market for higher education. There, especially at the high end of the market, demand exceeds supply at the stated price—year in and year out—by an enormous margin. At one small, high-quality liberal arts institution in the east, for example, 4,500 people apply each year for only 500 positions in the freshman class. At universities nearer the pinnacle of the academic pyramid, an even higher proportion of eager customers are routinely turned away. Yet despite this persistent excess demand, many universities charge students only about one-third of what it costs to serve them. This, needless to say, is a stark contrast with the pattern portrayed in economics textbooks.

The root cause of this difference is that hierarchy matters in the higher education market but is assumed not to matter in textbook markets

for ordinary goods and services (although, as I will presently note, hierarchy *does* increasingly matter in many actual markets for goods and services). Hierarchy in education is nothing new, of course, but it has become far more important than in the past.

One reason is that many labor markets have increasingly become what Duke economist Philip Cook and I have called "winner-take-all markets." These are markets in which small differences in performance (or even small differences in the credentials used to predict performance) translate into extremely large differences in pay. Such markets have long been familiar in entertainment and sports. The best soprano may be only marginally better than the second-best, but in a world in which most people listen to music on compact discs, the first may earn a seven-figure annual salary while the second struggles to get by.

In similar fashion, new technologies allow us to clone the services of the most talented performers in a growing number of occupations, thereby enabling them to serve ever broader and more lucrative markets. The market for tax advice, for example, was once served almost exclusively by a large army of local practitioners, but is increasingly served by the developers of a small handful of software programs.

Another important source of the winner-take-all payoff structure is that in many markets buyers care less about the absolute quality of the product itself than about how it compares with other products like it. This source, as we'll see, has special implications for the higher education market. But first let's look at how it affects the automobile market. Many aspects of the demand for cars are based strictly on the functional characteristics of the car. Does it start up when you turn the key? Does it get acceptable gas mileage? And so on. There is an increasingly important segment of this market, however, in which those characteristics are taken for granted as buyers search for something more. They want a fast car, or they want a car that handles well, or one that stands out from the crowd. These characteristics differ from fuel economy and reliability in that they are far more context-dependent. How fast does a car have to be to impress the potential buyer? If a car produced in 1925 could reach 60 m.p.h. *eventually*, the driver would experience it as breathtakingly exciting, a *really* fast car. Today if your car does not get from 0 to 60 m.p.h. in under 6 seconds, it doesn't seem like a fast car. Context-sensitive characteristics like speed and handling dictate an increasing share of purchase decisions in automobile markets. And when what people want is defined in sharply relative terms, only a limited number of suppliers can deliver. In the extreme case, only a single company can truthfully claim to offer the fastest car in the market.

Similar contextual issues have become increasingly important in the purchase of many high-end services. Suppose you were the CEO of a financially distressed corporation and were looking for advice from a management-consulting firm. Which firm should you hire: McKinsey— widely thought to be first among equals in the management consulting field—or some lesser-ranked firm that is considerably cheaper, yet, in absolute terms, nearly as good? You know that in either case the advice you get may not eliminate your firm's financial woes, in which case your board of directors will want to know why. If you had hired McKinsey, you could respond that you sought the best available advice and followed it. Critics might still second-guess you. But at the very least, you would be far less vulnerable to their charges than if you had hired some lesser-ranked firm. And if McKinsey's advice worked, no one would ever complain that you paid too much for it.

The upshot is that McKinsey and a handful of other elite management-consulting firms are essentially able to set extremely high prices and still attract more business than they can handle. As employers, such firms also have their pick of the most able college graduates. When they post positions, mail sacks full of résumés arrive in their personnel offices day after day. And no wonder. If a new recruit survives the early rounds and becomes a partner, she'll reap an annual salary of many hundreds of thousands of dollars.

That such salaries persistently attract an enormous surplus of applicants might seem to suggest that the elite consulting firms are paying far too much. Why don't they just offer less money and attract only the number

of qualified applicants they need? The answer is not that these firms have failed to grasp the elementary logic of supply and demand. On the contrary; they understand that a very different logic governs the hiring decisions of firms whose fate hinges on reputation and relative performance. These firms need the graduates of elite institutions just as much as those graduates need them. And the more applicants they attract, the better they do.

After all, they are selling advice, perhaps the most the most difficult of all services to evaluate. They send recruits who are barely out of college to advise seasoned professionals about what they should do with their businesses. Under the circumstances, establishing credibility is a tall order—perhaps an impossibly tall order for graduates of institutions with less than elite status. When the client knows that he is dealing with a graduate of an elite school, however, things are different. Every year more high school valedictorians apply to Stanford than there are positions in Stanford's freshman class, and the client knows that if he had applied to Stanford, he probably would have been rejected. Although this knowledge may operate completely below the level of conscious awareness, it nonetheless confers an unmistakable gloss on the advice given by the elite school graduate.

For present purposes, the important point is that even if McKinsey and the other elite consulting firms had time to interview everyone who submits an application, they would still have good reasons to confine their attention to the graduates of elite institutions. You might be exceedingly well qualified, but if you are not from one of these schools, odds are they won't talk to you.

The logic is essentially the same in many other winner-take-all labor markets. Want to be a top mergers-and-acquisitions attorney? Better graduate with honors from an elite law school. Want to be an investment banker? Better go to one of the top-ranked business schools.

Because of the growing premium for attending a top-ranked professional or graduate program, competition for admission into these programs has naturally become more intense. How can a student assure admission to such a program? In an earlier day, it was sufficient to compile a strong undergraduate record at almost any college or university. But no longer. A friend who teaches at Harvard described to me the case of a woman from a small Florida college who had applied to Harvard's graduate program in economics several years ago. She had scored within a few points of 800 on her GREs, both quantitative and verbal, and also had a very high score on the economics achievement test. She had straight A's and glowing recommendations from several senior professors, who described her as the best student they'd ever encountered. The admissions committee agonized long and hard over this woman's file, but in the end decided to reject her. They simply had too many other applicants who had compiled equally strong records at much more highly selective institutions.

Students, in short, confront an increasingly competitive environment. Between 1979 and 1989, the percentage of students who scored above 700 on the SAT verbal section and matriculated at one of the 33 "most competitive" schools on the Barron's list rose from 32 percent to 43 percent.

As more and more of the best students attend the most selective schools, the payoff for going to these schools gets ever higher. This is another respect in which the production of education is different from the production of an ordinary good or service. A university's customers are one of the inputs in the production of education. As a student, you want to be at a school where the other students are good, partly because you learn more, but also because that's increasingly where the best employers do their recruiting. Faculty, who have always liked working with good students, thus face similarly higher payoffs from affiliating with elite schools.

These multiple positive-feedback loops greatly increase the rewards for a university that succeeds in its efforts to command elite status. At the same time, they impose stiffer penalties on those that fail in their efforts. Success breeds success and failure breeds failure.

54

Universities thus face increasing pressure to bid for the various
resources that facilitate the quest for high rank in the educational
marketplace. Star faculty command ever higher salaries and require
ever more elaborate and costly support. No wonder, then, that
universities find themselves under increasingly intense financial
pressure despite the record growth in the value of their endowment
portfolios.

Let us consider, finally, how the new environment has shaped financial
aid decisions. From the university's perspective, the merit scholar is an
asset whose value has appreciated sharply. Someone who scored 750 on
both sections of the SAT always paid lower prices for admission to the
university than other students. But never before have we witnessed such
intense bidding to attract these students.

Think of yourself as the admissions director of a school that's trying to
move forward in the academic pecking order. On your desk sit the
folders for two applicants. They have almost the same credentials, but
one is just a little better than the other. She has a 4.2 average while
the other has a 3.8. She got 790 on both SATs while the other got only 700.
The applicant with better credentials comes from a family with an
annual income of $500,000, while the other student's family earns only
$30,000. Now, as in the past, you accept both students. In the past, your
financial aid package for these students would have been tailored in a
way that I think most of us would feel was just: The student from the
family with limited means would have gotten a large aid package, and
the student with no financial constraints would have gotten a much
smaller package, or more likely no aid at all. In today's climate,
however, such offers would almost guarantee that the better qualified
student would go elsewhere. And that would make your university less
attractive to other top students and faculty. In light of the feedback
loops just discussed, the indirect effects of failure to land even a single
top student can multiply manyfold. And this, in a nutshell, explains the
growing tendency for merit-based financial aid to displace need-based
financial aid.

Many elite institutions were once party to an agreement whereby they essentially pledged to target limited financial aid money for those students with the greatest financial needs. Not to put too fine a point on it, this was a cartel agreement to curb competition for students with elite credentials. Animated by its belief that unbridled competition always and everywhere leads to the best outcome, the Justice Department took a dim view of this agreement. And it brought an antitrust suit that led to the agreement's termination.

Once we appreciate the logic of the financial incentives that confront participants in winner-take-all markets, however, we may feel less inclined to embrace the mantra that all outcomes of open competition must be good. The problem is that when reward depends on rank, behavior that looks attractive to each individual often looks profoundly unattractive from the perspective of the group. Such behaviors I call "smart for one, dumb for all."

We see vivid illustrations of these behaviors in the animal kingdom. Consider the battles among male elk for access to females. This is a winner-take-all tournament, since the animals that defeat their rivals get a disproportionate share of mating opportunities, and the outcomes depend not on absolute fighting prowess but on relative prowess. In such situations, there's enormous Darwinian selection pressure in favor of traits or behaviors that confer even the slightest relative advantage. When a mutant elk with slightly larger antlers than its rivals appeared, it garnered far more than its share of mating opportunities, causing the genes for its bigger antlers to proliferate. Generation by generation, this led to gradually larger male antlers, so that male elks today often sport racks more than five feet wide.

Useful as these antlers may be in the battles between individual males, however, they are an enormous handicap from the perspective of male elks as a group. If a male with a five-foot rack of antlers is chased into the woods by predators, he's dead meat. If male elks could hold a referendum on a proposal requiring each animal's rack of antlers to be trimmed by half, the proposal would pass unanimously. After all, the

outcome of contests for mates would be unaffected and each animal would be far less likely to fall victim to predators.

Elks cannot hold town meetings, of course. But humans can, and do, as when universities colluded to prevent need-based aid from being driven out by competitive forces. Of course, cooperative agreements to limit competition can also cause harm, as in the notorious price-fixing cases of antitrust lore.

The challenge, of course, is to make informed distinctions. Antitrust authorities might consider a retreat from their uncritical belief that unlimited competition necessarily leads to the greatest good for all. Manifestly it does not. Collective agreements should be scrutinized not on quasi-religious grounds, but according to the practical test of whether they limit harmful effects of competition without compromising its many benign effects. In my view, the collective agreement among universities regarding financial aid policy clearly met this test.

The economic forces that give rise to winner-take-all markets are here to stay. No university, acting alone, can alter the extent to which these forces militate against need-based aid. There remain compelling ethical reasons for basing financial aid more heavily on need than on merit. Indeed, the growth in income and wealth inequality caused by spreading winner-take-all markets makes the case for need-based aid more compelling than ever. But if such aid is to survive in the long run, we must act collectively.

Robert H. Frank holds a joint appointment at Cornell University, as Professor of Economics in the Johnson Graduate School of Management and as the Goldwin Smith Professor of Economics, Ethics, and Public Policy in the College of Arts and Sciences, where he has taught since 1972. He has published on a variety of subjects, including price and wage discrimination, public utility pricing, the measurement of unemployment spell lengths, and the distributional consequences of direct foreign investment. For the past several years, his research has focused on rivalry and cooperation in economic and social behavior. His books include Choosing the Right Pond: Human Behavior and the Quest for Status *(Oxford University Press, 1985);* Passions Within Reason: The Strategic Role of the Emotions *(W.W. Norton, 1988); and* Microeconomics and Behavior *(McGraw-Hill, 1991).* The Winner Take All Society, *coauthored with Philip Cook (The Free Press, 1995), received a Critic's Choice Award, was named a Notable Book of the Year by the* New York Times, *and was included in* Business Week's *list of the ten best books of 1996 by the* China Times. *His latest book,* Luxury Fever: Money and Happiness in an Era of Excess, *was published by The Free Press in January 1999.*

Doing the Right Thing
in a Winner-Take-All World

Luncheon Address by Donald M. Stewart

Thanks, Don, for that kind introduction and for all of your hard work in preparing for this colloquium. As I am sure all of you recognize by now, Don Saleh's leadership has paid off in really exciting sessions at this event.

I accepted the invitation from Hal Higginbotham, which I knew had Don's blessing, to participate in this important colloquium with pleasure and great anticipation. Throughout my tenure at the College Board, the discussions and debates—the *colloquies*, if you will—within this important constituency have always been stimulating: vigorous, provocative, impassioned, and central to our mission.

I also accepted gladly the invitation to make these remarks because I respect and admire Hal's leadership and the excellent work that he and his staff colleagues undertake under very challenging conditions, in collaboration with the CSS Council and Assembly. The theme for this gathering is also one about which I happen to care a great deal. I do worry a little, however, that the title in the program—for one has to provide these captions in advance!—promises more than any speaker could really deliver. In retrospect, I wish we had at least made the title into a question rather than an assertion.... As in, "Is It Possible to Do the Right Thing?" or even, "What Is the Right Thing to Do in a Winner-Take-All World?" Because, in truth, I rise today with more questions than answers.

One cause for my hesitation is that—like the heads of so many educational organizations—I have never sat directly in your places nor had to make precisely the tough decisions—whom to admit, whom to aid—that define your professional lives. So, it is perhaps risky for me to rise at all and to give you advice on a subject that you know better than I.

But, yet I do so, and am actually eager for the opportunity, because my own professional life has been defined by certain experiences that add, I believe, legitimacy to my remarks.

As some of you know, I started down this path as a young man from the south side of Chicago who landed as a freshman at Grinnell College, thanks especially to parents who believed firmly in the value of education and acted accordingly. At Grinnell, I benefited from a wonderful liberal arts experience and interaction with faculty, fellow students, and administrators who cared about my academic success and general well-being.

My learning continued when I worked for the Ford Foundation in Africa and the Middle East, and saw reflected in other cultures the sharp contrasts between worlds of material affluence and those whose wealth was in the mirages of hope and aspiration.

Working for Martin Meyerson, the president of the University of Pennsylvania in the decade of the 70s, these pieces came together, as I began to understand what caused institutions—even stately, historic institutions like Penn—to move and to act. Later, at Spelman College in Atlanta, my role as president placed me in a constant cycle of reconciling multiple, often competing goals—the aspirations of faculty and their commitment to quality, the need to recruit students, the challenges inherent in helping families somehow pay for college, and the strong belief in equality on which that very special 118-year-old institution is grounded.

A few of those experiences have now come full circle. For more than 20 years, I have been a trustee of Grinnell College, and participated in extended debates about quality and enrollment, yield and discount, endowment and investment. As you may know, Grinnell has been especially fortunate with its endowment, thereby enabling difficult, but

wonderful choices.

And soon I will conclude more than a decade as the president of this wonderful association. Here at the College Board, I have had the opportunity to focus our attention on the twin goals of excellence and equity while also struggling with many of you through a period of gut-wrenching changes in financial aid policies and enrollment conventions.

At this juncture professionally, the following words of T.S. Eliot resonate quite personally. *In Four Quartets*, he wrote:

> We shall not cease from exploration
> And the end of all our exploring
> Will be to arrive where we started
> And know the place for the first time.

In that spirit, I hope you will indulge me in essaying forth on several core issues that define our mutual workspace.

From the Morrill Act through the G.I. Bill...from the Civil Rights Act through the first Basic Grants legislation...from the creation of the TRIO programs through the bipartisan support of student aid programs for more than a quarter-century...our nation has put its money where its mouth is when it comes to higher education.

We can and do argue about whether we ought to put still more money into higher education, or instead put it into different kinds of programs, or redistribute it differently across the population.

But the fact remains that as a society, we have made a more concentrated, sustained commitment to educating our people, all our people, than any nation on earth. With good reason, other countries envy and seek to emulate what we have done.

Why is it, then, that nobody *here*—either in this room or in the country at large—seems satisfied? How is it that for all our expenditure of human and material capital, for all the effort of so many people of great talent and good will, our national educational enterprise often appears to be tearing at the seams? Indeed, some days it appears that there is little or no sense of national enterprise left at all—just individuals and institutions looking out for their own narrowly-defined self-interest.

Nicholas Lemann, national correspondent for the *Atlantic Monthly*, seems to confirm that notion on an even larger scale in a piece he published last fall in the *New York Times Magazine* entitled, "The New American Consensus: Government of, by and for the Comfortable." Lemann writes that

> the idea is that government should serve the ordinary, hard-working individual—providing safety, public goods like roads and parks and the tools necessary to seek opportunity, like education. It should protect people from unfair or excessive aspects of the marketplace.... But that's it. The consensus represents a national embrace of a kind of one-way libertarianism. Its main assumption is that the government has a very serious obligation to the middle class.... On the other hand, the middle class is in no way obligated to commit time or money to larger national projects....

Neither I nor Lemann would mean to negate some very real achievements. It's been more than 30 years since the Civil Rights Act was passed, since Charlayne Hunter-Gault and the late Hamilton Holmes were admitted (albeit under court order) to the University of Georgia, since President Lyndon Johnson signed his name to Executive Order 11246 and launched an idea called "affirmative action."

And it is certainly true that more of our citizens than ever are completing high school and going on to postsecondary education. It has been more than 20 years since women closed the gender gap in higher education. There has also been at least some growth in the rate of college attendance across all socioeconomic groups. And the prowess of our institutions has steadily advanced.

But the rest of the story isn't nearly so encouraging. Low-income 18- to 24-year-olds attend college at a much lower rate than their peers at higher income levels. In fact, the participation gap today remains about as wide as it was in 1970.

Furthermore, Mike McPherson (President of Macalaster College and a College Board Trustee) and Morty Schapiro (Dean of the College of Letters, Arts, and Sciences at USC) have demonstrated that students from the least advantaged backgrounds are concentrating themselves in two-year institutions.

I want to be clear: That is no criticism of community colleges. Far from it! It is to their credit that they continue to make opportunities so widely available.

But it cannot be good news that low-income students have increasingly gravitated *to* community colleges over the same two-decade period in which upper- and middle-income students have gravitated *away* from them. A postsecondary educational enterprise bifurcated so sharply along socioeconomic lines is surely not the outcome that anyone committed to equal opportunity—in education, or in work, or in life— would want. Our educational quality suffers from its inequality.

Nor is there much good news to be found in our colleague Tom Mortenson's compelling analysis of educational attainment rates and family socioeconomic status. Not only do minority and low-income students enroll in postsecondary education at lower rates than middle- and upper-income students, but those who do aspire and do enroll are far less likely to persist and succeed.

Despite billions upon billions of dollars of need-based aid, only 6 percent of the least economically advantaged students earn a bachelor's degree within five years of initial enrollment, compared with more than 40 percent of their counterparts at the highest income levels. Again, our collective educational quality suffers from its inequality.

And even after nearly 30 years of affirmative action, African-American and Hispanic students are still far less likely to earn a bachelor's degree than white and Asian students. In a labor market where credentials *matter*, this persistent inequity threatens not just our economic competitiveness, but social stability.

In a provocative article in last summer's issue of the *College Board Review*, Larry Gladieux—who is here with us today and has argued virtually all his professional life that there isn't enough financial aid—makes a persuasive case, with his colleague Scott Swail, that financial aid alone just isn't enough, because a dropout with a student loan to repay is probably in worse shape than someone who never enrolled at all.

Gladieux and Swail argue vigorously that the nation must find a way to expand programs, particularly direct outreach, intervention, and mentoring programs, that influence students' motivation and academic preparation.

Our national educational quality suffers from our persistent educational inequality.

Well, that's the situation at one end of the socioeconomic spectrum in the waning days of the twentieth century. It is not hard to understand why folks at the bottom of the heap are so unhappy. But why aren't the people higher up the ladder happier, especially since it would seem that they have everything that is denied to those at the bottom?

For one thing, despite a marked slowing of the pace in recent years, especially among independent colleges, tuition increases continue to outstrip both inflation and growth in both personal and family incomes.

At the very farthest end of the spectrum, of course, that's less true. In an era of the richer getting richer, there are still families who can finance their children's aspirations without substantially sacrificing their style of living or level of consumption. They may not *choose* to do so, but they *can* do so if they choose.

But for the much broader band of population that comprises America's middle class, it requires more than a stretch—it takes great, wrenching contortions that can tear at the fabric of family and erode cherished dreams of comfortable living and secure retirement.

These families have some discretionary income, too—not necessarily enough to pay the full price of a college education at the most expensive institutions, or at least, not out of current income alone. But they are nevertheless people with choices.

They are also good, informed, well-educated consumers, accustomed to searching out the best deals and sniffing out the stinkers. Now, parents obsessing about their toddlers' admissibility to the "right" preschool may be the stuff of TV sitcoms. But it's a lot less funny when those same parents are pressuring their children—and their children's teachers— for higher grades because they're worried about their admissibility to college down the road.

Or when they're shelling out hundreds of dollars for test-prep courses and college consultants, or ghostwriting their children's admissions essays, or "negotiating" with colleges about the terms of their enrollment as though they were agents and their children professional athletes or movie stars.

But, truth be told, we in higher education have often been part of the problem for these students and families—instead of part of the solution. We have, ostensibly to be efficient and to survive, imported powerful commercial concepts into higher education—positioning strategies and marketing tactics, price discrimination, and leveraging—sometimes acting as though seats in our classrooms and space in our dorms are seats on airplanes, or, even worse, cabins on boats which we fear will surely sink if these commercial tactics are not applied.

We can hardly blame the people we treat like customers if they *act* like customers. (And it bears mentioning, too, that we have been pretty selective about which marketing concepts we've chosen to adopt. Would that we had all spent as much energy on adding value to our product as we have on its pricing and promotion!)

Increasingly, I have the sense that, to paraphrase Yeats, the center is simply not holding. All too much of the time, the videotape seems to reveal every family for itself, every institution for itself, and *caveat emptor, caveat vendor*—on both sides of the table. Of course, that's for the families and the institutions that actually come together at the table at all. In a winner-take-all world, there are far too many of our fellow citizens who aren't even getting a glimpse of the table.

Someone once suggested to me—on a wholly different topic—that when dissatisfaction is pretty evenly distributed over the whole range of people with a stake in a particular situation, it's probably an indication that we've got it about as right as we can get it.

I've given that idea a lot of thought and concluded that the observation is often true. Certainly, it's always a good cocktail-party line. But in this particular case, I think it's a recipe for disaster, and that the time has come to pause and take stock. We are on the verge of forgetting—as both providers and consumers—that our educational enterprise is held together by a fragile public consensus, one in which all of the stakeholders are able to get a return from the system to which we all contribute.

All of which means that we haven't yet "gotten it" as right as it has to be for higher education to prosper in the next millennium. As we think about what it would take, I would commend two important pieces of theoretical work for your attention. First, Derek Bok and Bill Bowen have given us—in the research supporting *Shape of the River*—enhanced ways to think about the value of affirmative action and diversity, both to individuals and to educational institutions. They have made it very clear that there is concrete value in looking beyond a narrow, near-term calculus.

And Sandy Baum (professor of economics at Skidmore and consulting economist to FASSAC) has articulated an elegant argument that efficiency and equity can be not only compatible, but that they represent complementary principles in the allocation of financial aid.

All three of these distinguished policy analysts would, I suspect, say that it is not only possible, but essential, to do the right thing in a winner-

take-all world. I suspect that many of you believe that, too, or you wouldn't be here grappling with these issues today.

The real challenge, of course, lies in discerning what the right thing is. Sandy Baum's call for "hard heads and soft hearts" is (like so much of what she says) right on point.

I don't have a comprehensive cure for what ails us in higher education, but let me suggest at least three elements of a prescription. Some of these thoughts may sound familiar to you, for they are built upon concepts that I first advanced at our 1995 National Forum in San Diego where I talked about the past, present, and future of affirmative action.

On that occasion, I urged us to make choices; my exhortation to you today is that we not only choose, but also act on those choices.

First, we should *choose to engage in the struggle* to make education better—for all students. This is, first and foremost, a matter of believing in our young people—in their aspirations and in their intrinsic value, to themselves, to their families, and to our democratic society.

It is arguing for a raised bar, for elevated educational standards that will serve to prepare our children—all of them—more effectively for college and for work. It is impressing accountability outcomes on K-12, not for political reasons or to satisfy some invidious investment calculus, but for the sake of the children who will benefit from those high standards. It also means adopting accountability outcomes for our own institutions of higher education as a reciprocal measure, in part as recognition of society's trust in us, but more to insure that we also serve these students well, that we truly add value to their lives.

Second, we should *choose to be fair.* In the first place, we simply cannot afford *not* to be fair. The fact is that we work for protected institutions, and fairness—i.e., concern for the larger world—is an essential part of the social compact on which we rely and to which we must contribute.

Yes, we do face many pressures and challenges, but society exempts us from yet many others, precisely because we do something special for society and its young people. Public colleges are, in a legal and political sense, organs of society, existing at the pleasure of taxpayer dollars. Private colleges, by virtue of the tax benefits they receive, not to mention direct and indirect funding streams that accrue to them, are also comparatively protected.

And we *owe* something to society in return for these privileges. That, in fact, was one key argument in favor of need-based aid raised in the financial aid antitrust litigation. Indeed, again as Sandy Baum notes, fairness remains a fundamental building block for our social structures because, without an adequate measure of it, everyone feels at risk and vulnerable.

Finally, we have every reason to *refuse to choose* between those values that ought not be separated. Just as Sandy Baum tells us we don't have to choose between equity and interdependent efficiency, we don't have to choose between equity and educational excellence.

The immediate past chair of our Board of Trustees and chair of the search committee for my successor, President Peter Stanley of Pomona College, puts an even sharper point on it. In a valedictory word delivered at our annual trustees retreat earlier this month in Puerto Rico, he reminded us that "we *dare not choose* between excellence and equity." Moral imperative and enlightened self-interest make it possible and necessary for us to hold both values dear and to drive toward them both, not toward one to the exclusion of the other.

I would never suggest to you that the issues are simple, or that the solutions to the problems we face are easy to envision, let alone execute. There is no easy formula to use in resolving these ambiguities and conflicts. But no one is in a better position than each of us to act, in our respective individual, institutional, social, and political spheres.

That's because we are, after all, educators, and many among us are

parents as well. *We are the people who see the power of learning to change the lives of our children.* In a democratic society so in need of intellectual and moral sustenance, we work to liberate lives by the freeing of minds and hearts. Let's return to T. S. Eliot, who put it this way:

> It is in fact a part of the function of education to help us escape—not from our own time, for we are bound by that—but from the intellectual and emotional limitations of our own time.

That is one very right thing we can now do, for whatever the economic world, in the end, we want to build a system in which all the participants can win.

I thank you for your indulgence, and wish you all Godspeed. ∎

List of Participants

Name of Institution	Name	Title
Agnes Scott College	Stephanie Balmer	Associate VP of Admission and Financial Aid
Amherst College	Joe Paul Case	Dean of Financial Aid
Boston College	Bob Lay	Dean of Enrollment Management
Boston College	Bernie Pekala	Director of Financial Strategies
Boston University	Barbara E. Tornow	Executive Director of Financial Assistance
Bowdoin College	Walter H. Moulton	Director of Student Aid
Bowdoin College	Stephen H. Joyce	Associate Director of Student Aid
Brown University	Mike Bartini	Director of Financial Aid
Bryn Mawr College	Nancy Monnich	Director of Admissions and Financial Aid
Bryn Mawr College	Gail Tatum	Director of Public Information
Bullis School	Sharon Alston	Director of College Counseling
California Institute of Technology	Charlene Liebau	Director of Admissions
Carleton College	Leonard M. Wenc	Director of Student Financial Services
City University of New York	George Chin	University Director Of Student Financial Assistance
Claremont McKenna College	Georgette DeVeres	Director of Financial Aid
Claremont McKenna College	Richard Vos	Dean of Admission and Financial Aid
COFHE	Kay Hanson	President
COFHE	Jim Monks	Senior Economist
Colby College	T. Steve Thomas	Director of Admissions
Colby College	Lucia Whittelsey	Director of Financial Aid
Colgate University	Marcelle Tyburski	Director of Student Aid
The College Board	Fred Dietrich	Senior Vice President for Programs and Development
The College Board	Kathleen Little	Executive Director, Financial Aid Services
The College Board	William Cavanaugh	Executive Director, Profile Processing
The College Board	Cynthia Bailey	Executive Director, Education Finance Services
The College Board	Bill Miller	College Scholarship Service
The College Board	Jim Slattery	Director of Financial Aid Services
The College Board	Jack Joyce	Manager, CSS Communications & Training
The College Board	Dorothy Sexton	Director, CSS Administration
The College Board	Harry Layman	Executive Director, Software Services
The College Board	Lawrence E. Gladieux	Executive Director for Policy Analysis
The College Board	Ken Brown	Vice President and Treasurer ·
The College Board	John Childers	Vice President for Communications & Government Relations
The College Board	Hal Higginbotham	Vice President Student Assistance Services
The College Board	Don Stewart	President
The College Board	Deb Schmidt	Consultant
The College Board	Bradley J. Quinn	Executive Director, Admissions, Enrollment & Information Services
The College Board	Alex Nichols	Executive Director, Corporate Marketing
The College Board	Carol Barker	V. P. of Associational Affairs & Secretary of the Corporation
The College Board	Gretchen W. Rigol	V. P., Guidance, Access & Assessment Services
College of Wooster	David Miller	Director of Financial Aid
Colorado School of Mines	Mary Davis	Associate Director of Financial Aid
Colorado School of Mines	Roger Koester	Director of Financial Aid
Columbia University	David Charlow	Associate Dean of Student Affairs
Convent of the Sacred Heart	Mary S. Jemail	Director of College Guidance
Cornell University	Nancy Meislahn	Director of Undergraduate Admissions
Cornell University	Donald Saleh	Dean of Admission and Financial Aid
Cornell University	Thomas Keane	Director of Financial Aid and Student Employment
Cornell University	Robert Frank	Goldwin Smith Professor of Economics
Dartmouth College	Virginia Hazen	Director of Financial Aid
Davidson College	Kathleen Stevenson-McNeely	Senior Associate Dean of Admission and Financial Aid
Davidson College	Dr. Nancy J. Cable	Dean of Admission and Financial Aid
Dickinson College	Judith B. Carter	Director of Financial Aid
Duke University	James A. Belvin	Director of Financial Aid
Duke University	Patricia H. Bogart	Senior Associate Director of Financial Aid
Edinburg High School	Eduardo Moreno	Financial Aid Officer
Edinburg High School	Reymundo Ramos	Financial Aid Officer
Emmanuel College	Anna Kelly	Director of Financial Aid
Emory University	Julia Perreault	Director of Financial Aid

Emory University	Daniel C. Walls	Dean of Admissions
Georgetown University	Patricia McWade	Dean of Student Financial Services
Georgetown University	Charles A. Deacon	Dean of Admissions
Hamilton College	Richard Fuller	Dean of Admission & Financial Aid
Hamilton College	Ken Kogut	Director of Financial Aid
Hampshire College	Audrey Y. Smith	Director of Admissions
Hampshire College	Kathleen Methot	Director of Financial Aid
Harvard and Radcliffe Colleges	Jim Miller	Director of Financial Aid
Harvey Mudd College	Youlonda Copeland-Morgan	Associate VP of Admission and Financial Aid
Hobart & William Smith Colleges	Don Emmons	Dean of Admissions and Financial Aid
Illinois Institute of Technology	David Jeitner	Associate Director of Admissions
Illinois Wesleyan University	Lynn Nichelson	Director of Financial Aid
Johns Hopkins University	Ellen Frishberg	Director of Student Financial Services
Johns Hopkins University	Robert J. Massa	Dean of Enrollment
Kalamazoo College	Joellen Silberman	Dean of Enrollment
Lafayette College	Barry McCarty	Dean of Enrollment Services
Lafayette College	Arlina B. DeNardo	Director of Financial Aid
Lehigh University	Lorna J. Hunter	Dean of Admissions
Lehigh University	William E. Stanford	Director of Financial Aid
Loyola College	Mark L. Lindenmeyer	Director of Financial Aid
Loyola Marymount University	Donna M. Palmer	Director of Financial Aid
Loyola Marymount University	Joseph A. Merante	Associate VP/Academic Affairs
Macalester College	Lorne Robinson	Dean of Admissions and Financial Aid
Macalester College	David Busse	Director of Financial Aid
Maguire Associates	Mary Ann Rowan	Senior Vice President
Marian College	John. E Shelton	Assistant Dean of Financial Aid & Enrollment Management
Meredith College	Sue Kearney	Dean, Enrollment Planning & Institutional Research
Meredith College	Dr. La Rose Spooner	Vice President for Marketing
Meredith College	Phillip Roof	Director of Financial Aid
Middlebury College	Robert Donaghey	Director of Financial Aid
Middlebury College	Michael Schoenfeld	Dean of Enrollment Planning
Middlebury College	Patricia Santner	Associate Director of Financial Aid
Mount Holyoke College	Jill Cashman	Director of Financial Assistance
Mount Holyoke College	Diane Anci	Acting Director of Admissions
Mount St. Mary's College	Jack Millis	Associate Director of Student Financing
Mount St. Mary's College	Katy Murphy	Executive Director of Enrollment
Nat'l Assoc. of Independent Schools	Mark Mitchell	Director, Financial Aid Services
Nazareth College	Bruce C. Woolley	Director of Financial Aid
Nazareth College	Tom Darin	Dean of Admissions
N.C. State Ed. Assist. Authority	Steven Brooks	Executive Director
N.C. State Ed. Assist. Authority	Elizabeth McDuffie	Asst. Director of Education, Training & Outreach
North Park University	John M. Baworowsky	VP for Admission & Financial Aid
Northwestern University	Carolyn Lindley	Director of Financial Aid
Northwestern University	Patsy Myers Emery	Senior Associate Director of Financial Aid
Oberlin College	Howard Thomas	Director of Financial Aid
Otterbein College	Tom Stein	Vice President for Enrollment
Pine Crest School	Marcia Hunt	Director of College Counseling
Plymouth Public Schools	Warren Valentine	Guidance Coordinator
Pomona College	Bruce Poch	Dean of Admissions
Pomona College	Pat Coy	Director of Financial Aid
Princeton University	Don Betterton	Director of Financial Aid
Providence College	Herb D'Arcy	Executive Director of Financial Aid
Providence College	Christopher Lydon	Dean of Enrollment Management
Rice University	Richard N. Stabell	Dean of Admission and Records
Saint Anselm College	Robert Andrea	Associate Director of Admissions
Saint Leo College	Gary Bracken	Dean of Admission and Financial Aid
Saint Mary's College	Mary Nucciarone	Director of Financial Aid
Saint Mary's College	Mary Pat Nolan	Director of Admissions
San Francisco Univ. H. S.	Christiane Neuville	Director of College Counseling
Santa Clara University	Annette Schmeling, RSCJ	Director of Undergraduate Admissions
Scannell & Kurz, Inc.	James Scannell	President
Skidmore College	Mary Lou W. Bates	Director of Admissions
Skidmore College	Sandy Baum	Professor of Economics

Appendix C
List of Participants

Skidmore College	Robert D. Shorb	Director of Student Aid & Family Finance
Skidmore College	Kent Jones	Dean of Enrollment and College Relations
Smith College	Myra Smith	Director of Financial Aid
Smith College	Nanci Tessier	Director of Admissions
Smith College	Ann Wright	Chief of Public Affairs
Stanford University	Cynthia Hartley Rife	Director of Student Awards
Stevens Institute of Technology	Maureen P. Weatherall	VP for Enrollment Management
SUNY System Administration	Alan E. Young	Director of School/College Relations
SUNY System Administration	John Curtice	Asst. Vice Chancellor for Student Affairs & Financial Aid Services
Swarthmore College	Laura Talbot	Director of Financial Aid
Transylvania University	David Cecil	Director of Financial Aid
Tufts University	David D. Cuttino	Dean of Undergraduate Admissions and Enrollment
Tufts University	Bill Eastwood	Director of Financial Aid
Tulane University	Elaine L. Rivera	Director of Financial Aid
University of Arkansas	Arlene Cash	Director of Undergraduate Admissions
University of Chicago	Theodore O'Neill	Dean of College Admissions
University of Chicago	Alicia Reyes	Director of College Aid
University of Maryland	Linda Clement	Assistant V. P. & Dir. Of Undergraduate Admissions
University of MA at Amherst	Kenneth Burnham	Associate Dean & Interim Director of Financial Aid
University of Miami	Paul Orehovec	Vice Provost & Dean of Enrollment
University of Michigan	Michael Nettles	Professor of Education
University of NC, Chapel Hill	Jerry Lucido	Director of Admission
University of Notre Dame	Joseph A. Russo	Director of Financial Aid
University of Notre Dame	Daniel J. Saracino	Assistant Provost for Enrollment
University of Pennsylvania	Lee Stetson	Dean of Admissions
University of Pennsylvania	William Schilling	Senior Director, Student Financial Services
University of Rochester	Andrea C. A. Leithner	Director of Financial Aid
University of San Diego	Warren Muller	Director of Enrollment Management
University of San Diego	Judith Lewis Logue	Director of Financial Aid Services
University of San Francisco	Susan Murphy	Associate Dean/Director of Financial Aid
University of San Francisco	BJ Johnson	Dean of Academic Services
University of San Francisco	Bill Henley	Associate Dean/Director Of Admission
University of Southern California	Joe Allen	Vice Provost for Enrollment
University of Southern California	Catherine Thomas	Associate Dean of Enrollment Services/ Director of Financial Aid
University of Texas at Arlington	Judy Schneider	Director of Financial Aid
University of the Pacific	Lynn Fox	Assoc. Dean of Enrollment Services/ Director of Financial Aid
University of Tulsa	Davis Gruen	Director of Student Financial Services
University of Wisconsin, Madison	Steve Van Ess	Director of Financial Aid
Vanderbilt University	David D. Mohning	Director of Student Financial Aid
Wabash College	Clint Gasaway	Director of Financial Aid
Wake Forest University	William G. Starling	Director of Admissions
Wake Forest University	William Wells	Director of Financial Aid
Washington and Lee University	William M. Hartog	Dean of Admission & Financial Aid
Washington and Lee University	John H. Decourcey	Director of Financial Aid
Washington College	Kevin Coveney	Vice President of Admissions
Washington College	Jean Narcum	Director of Student Aid
Washington University	Ben Sandler	Vice Chancellor for Financial Policy
Wellesley College	Patricia Ramonat	Senior Associate Director of Financial Aid
Wellesley College	Kathryn Osmond	Director of Financial Aid
Wellesley College	Janet Lavin Rapelye	Dean of Admission
The Wellington School	Stuart R. Oremus	Director of College Counseling
The Westminster School	Wade Boggs	College Counselor
The Westminster School	Juan J. Egues	College Scholarship/ Financial Aid Counselor
Wesleyan University	Edwin Below	Project Manager, SFIS
Wheaton College	Robin Randall	Associate Dean of Student Financial Services
Wheaton College	Gail Berson	Dean of Admissions
Williams College	Phil Wick	Director of Financial Aid
Yale University	Donald Routh	University Director of Financial Aid

College Scholarship Service® Council, 1998-99

Donald A. Saleh, Chair
Dean of Admissions and Financial Aid
Cornell University

Georgette DeVeres, Chair-Elect
Associate Dean, Director of Financial Aid
Claremont McKenna College

Steven E. Brooks, Past Chair
Executive Director
North Carolina State Education Assistance Authority

Pat Coye
Director of Financial Aid
Pomona College

Andrew Gooden
Student
Samuel Gompers Vocational-Technical High School
Bronx, New York

Christina M. Knickerbocker
Director of Student Financial Aid & Employment
State University of New York at Binghamton

Ronald T. Laszewski
Director of Financial Aid
Bucknell University

Evangeline B. Manjares
Assistant Dean of Students for Financial Aid
Nassau Community College

Thomas A. Scarlett
Director, Office of Financial Aid
Michigan State University

Michael H. Scott
Director of Scholarships & Student Financial Aid
Texas Christian University

Kate L. Sutton
Student
Hope College
Eaton Rapids, Michigan

James M. Swanson
Director of Financial Aid
The Colorado College

Miguel Brito
Director of Guidance and Testing
Dwight-Englewood School

Joe Paul Case
Dean of Financial Aid
Amherst College

David Cecil
Director of Financial Aid
Transylvania University

William R. McClintock, Jr.
Director of College Counseling
The Mercersburg Academy

Cynthia Monaco
Guidance Counselor
Robert E. Lee High School
San Antonio, Texas

Carol Mowbray
College Coordinator of Student and Support Services
Northern Virginia Community College

Lynn Nichelson
Director of Financial Aid
Illinois Wesleyan University

Shirley A. Ort
Assoc. Vice Chancellor & Director, Scholarships & Student Aid
University of North Carolina-Chapel Hill

Laura Talbot
Director of Financial Aid
Swarthmore College

Howard Thomas
Director of Financial Aid
Oberlin College

Lucia W. Whittelsey
Director of Financial Aid
Colby College

Ann Elizabeth Therese Young
Student
Marian High School
Omaha, Nebraska

College Scholarship Service Council Financial Aid Standards and Services Committee, 1998-99

Edwin Below, Chair
Project Manager
Student Information System
Wesleyan University

Youlonda Copeland-Morgan, Vice Chair
Associate Vice President of
Admission and Financial Assistance
Harvey Mudd College

David Charlow
Director of Financial Aid
Columbia University

Stanley G. Hudson
Senior Associate Dean
Massachusetts Institute of Technology

Mark Lindenmeyer
Director of Financial Aid
Loyola College

Julie Rice Mallette
Director of Financial Aid
North Carolina State University

Mary Nucciarone
Director of Financial Aid
St. Mary's College

Donna Palmer
Director of Financial Aid
Loyola Marymount University

Bernard Pekala
Director of Financial Strategies
Boston College

Elaine Rivera
Director of Financial Aid
Tulane University

William Schilling
Senior Director, Financial Aid
University of Pennsylvania